BLUE BOOK 5

Fred J. Schonell
Phyllis Flowerdew

Oliver & Boyd

Acknowledgments

We are grateful to the following for supplying photographs and giving permission for their reproduction in this book:

Heather Angel (p. 132); BBC Hulton Picture Library (p. 95, foot); British Hovercraft Corporation (p. 118, foot); Camera Press London (pp. 21, 23—photos by S. K. Dutt); The J. Allan Cash Photo Library (p. 39); John Cleare/Mountain Camera (cover); Colorsport (p. 133); Cunard Line (p. 118, top); Eric and David Hosking (pp. 92, 93, 130 (photo by A. R. Thompson)); Frank W. Lane (p. 94—photo by Ronald Thompson); The Mansell Collection (p. 79); Picturepoint—London (pp. 40, 128); Rex Features (pp. 20, 141); Royal Geographical Society (pp. 51, 53); Royal National Lifeboat Institution (p. 119, foot); Roy Shaw (p. 131); Shell International Petroleum Co Ltd (p. 119, top); Frank Spooner Pictures (pp. 19, 22); Topham (p. 95).

Illustrated by Shirley Bellwood, Tony Herbert, Nicholas Hewetson, Alexa Rutherford, Michael Strand and George Woodford.

Oliver & Boyd
Longman House
Burnt Mill
Harlow
Essex CM20 2JE
An Imprint of Longman Group UK Ltd

First published 1949
Fourth edition 1985
Eighth impression 1992

© Phyllis Flowerdew and the Executors of the late Sir Fred J. Schonell 1965, 1985. (Except 'Mother Teresa' and 'The Seventh Climb' © Moira Miller 1985 and 'Bjorn Borg' © Anne Forsyth 1985.) All rights reserved; no part of this publication may be reproduced, stored in a retrieval system, or transmitted in any form or by any means, electronic, mechanical, photocopying, recording, or otherwise without either the prior written permission of the Publishers or a licence permitting restricted copying in the United Kingdom issued by the Copyright Licensing Agency Ltd, 90 Tottenham Court Road, London, W1P 9HE.

ISBN 0 05 003747 1

Set in 12/18pt Monophoto Plantin 110
Printed in Hong Kong
SWT/08

Preface

The Wide Range Readers are planned to provide graded reading practice for junior school children. Because children of 7–11 have a wide range of reading needs and attainments, there are three parallel series—Blue, Green and Red books—to provide plenty of material to suit the interests and reading ages of every child.

Books 1–4 are graded by half yearly reading ages, for use by appropriate groups within a class. Book 1 should provide an easy read for children with a reading age of about $7-7\frac{1}{2}$. Children with reading ages below 7 are recommended to use the Wide Range Starters.

The controlled vocabulary of the series makes the books suitable for the following reading ages:

$6\frac{1}{2}-7$	**Starter Books**—Blue, Green and Red
$7-7\frac{1}{2}$	**Book 1**—Blue, Green and Red
$7\frac{1}{2}-8$	**Book 2**—Blue, Green and Red
$8-8\frac{1}{2}$	**Book 3**—Blue, Green and Red
$8\frac{1}{2}-9$	**Book 4**—Blue, Green and Red
$9+$	**Book 5**—Blue, Green and Red
$10+$	**Book 6**—Blue, Green and Red
$11+$	**Book 7**—Red only
$12+$	**Book 8**—Red only

Contents

page

- 5 **The Ski Race**
- 17 **Mother Teresa**
- 24 **Grandfather's Ship**
- 34 **Eros**
- 40 **The Seventh Climb**
- 56 **When Anna Danced**
- 68 **Reynard**
- 76 **The Boy Who Liked Music**
- 80 **Star Patterns**
- 82 **The Jar of Olives**
- 93 **Did You Know This?**
- 96 **Deno All Alone**
- 110 **Do You Know?**
- 112 **The Story of Ships**
- 120 **The Story of a Road**
- 130 **Do You Know?**
- 133 **Bjorn Borg**

The Ski Race

Down the snow-covered mountain side went Franz on skis. So swiftly he went, that from the distance he looked almost like a bird flying past. The wind met him in a little rush, and his skis sent tiny fountains of powdered snow into the air.

Franz was ten years old, and he had learnt to ski almost as soon as he had learnt to walk, for his home had always been high up in the mountains of Austria.

He rested a moment, and looked down below at the dark green fir trees laden with snow. Beyond the trees he could see the village with its wooden houses nestling in the valley, and the morning sun glinting on the windows of the painted church. Summer in

Austria was lovely, but winter was almost too beautiful to be true.

On the westward slopes people were moving about —small and far away—putting red flags in the snow. They were getting the course ready for the ski races. Franz smiled. This was the most important day of his life. This afternoon at three o'clock the ski races were to begin. His name was down on the list for children under twelve. Oh, if only he could win! The village children were very fast. They had played and practised together every week-end for months. Franz usually had to practise alone, for his sister was only a baby, and his house was far from the village. But he was fast too, and he knew that if everything went well, he ought to win. He did want to win. He wanted to win the ski race more than anything else in the world!

But no. There was one thing he wanted even more than that. He wanted to meet Karl Engels. Karl Engels was the champion skier of Austria, and the holder of the speed record for Europe. How wonderful it would be to see him—to speak to him! Franz sighed.

"I'll practise once more," he said to himself, "and then I'll go indoors and rest."

He pretended that this was the actual race, and that

the baby fir tree just ahead was the winning post. Away he went. The wind met him in a little rush, and his skis left a smooth narrow track in the snow behind him. He pretended that Karl Engels waited at the winning post. And when Franz passed the baby fir tree, and won the pretend race, Karl came forward and shook hands and said,

"That was a fine bit of skiing, Franz!" If only such a thing would really happen!

* * * * * *

At dinner time Franz's mother said,

"You'll go directly after dinner, won't you, Franz. Then you'll have time to rest before the race starts."

"Yes, Mother." His eyes shone with excitement, for it was nearly time for the race at last.

"I'm sorry I can't come to watch you," went on Mother, "but Father is too ill to be left alone."

"Yes. I'm sorry too."

"Never mind. You'll be able to tell me all about it when you come back."

"Do you think I'll win, Mother?"

"I shouldn't be at all surprised. You've worked hard,

and you're fast for your age. Why, one day you might become the champion skier of Austria, and the holder of the speed record for Europe!"

"Oh, yes!"

These pleasant thoughts were interrupted by a voice from upstairs.

"Father's calling," said Franz. "Shall I go to him?"

"No. You finish your dinner." Mother went out of the room, and Franz heard the sound of her footsteps on the wooden stairs. Poor Father! He had been ill so long. He must be tired of lying in bed all day when the sun was shining and the snow was gleaming. How he must long to be up, and doing his work again.

In the summer Franz's father was a mountain guide, and in the winter he gave skiing lessons on the slopes above the village.

He had other work too. He had to look after the hut near the mountain top, because his house was nearest to it.

The hut was stout and strong, and its door was always left unlocked, so that anyone wandering up there in the heights could walk in at any time and shelter for the night. There was a way across the mountains from the east, and in the summer climbers came with rucksacks and ropes and ice axes, and the hut was often used. Travellers always found bunks and blankets for sleeping, a lamp for light, and pots and pans, a can of oil, and a stove for cooking. Franz's father went up from time to time to see that everything was all right, and to take more oil to put into the can.

In winter he didn't go so often, for the hut had fewer visitors. But even so, there were men making ski tours across the mountains, sleeping in different huts each night, trying out their strength, and watching the white beauty of winter in the peaks.

Suddenly Mother came into the room again. She looked worried.

"Oh, Franz," she said. "Someone will have to take oil up to the hut."

Franz sat quite still. Fancy forgetting the hut!

Father had not been there for weeks and weeks. The oil must be getting low. Surely the can must be empty by now. Skiers would arrive, cold and tired and hungry. They wouldn't be able to light the lamp, or use the stove to cook their food. *Someone* would have to take oil up for them.

"Tomorrow," thought Franz. But tomorrow might be too late. People might arrive at the hut tonight, and find no oil.

"It's the ski race today," said Franz in a whisper.

"I know," murmured Mother, and she looked so unhappy that Franz turned his eyes away.

"I can't leave Father," said Mother softly. From upstairs came the sound of Father coughing. The baby awoke from sleep and began to cry.

"I'll go to the hut, Mother," said Franz. "I know the way. I went twice last summer with Father."

"It's harder in the winter, and there's no time to get there and back today."

"I can stay the night in the hut, and return home early in the morning."

"You'll miss the ski race," murmured Mother.

"It doesn't matter," said Franz. "It doesn't matter a bit."

But of course it did matter, and Franz felt very sad as he packed his rucksack with food for supper and breakfast, fastened the can of oil to his back, and fixed his skis to his feet.

"Goodbye," he said.

His mother, holding the baby, watched him go. He was a good skier. She wasn't worried about that. He was a good climber too, and the way up from this side was really quite easy. But he would miss the ski race —and he looked small to be going up there in the clouds alone.

Franz followed a little path through a patch of fir trees, where the snow was crisp and hard like ice, and his progress was slow because he had to dig his skis in sideways on the slope. Then, when he had passed the trees, he travelled across the mountain and back again in wide zig-zag tracks, each one above the one before it. A sound came to his ears—the sound of distant shouting and cheering. The ski races had started. He had practised so hard. He had looked forward to the ski race for so long, and now he was missing it. This was to have been the most important day of his life, and now it was spoiled.

That afternoon, just as the sun went down, Franz

reached the hut. All alone in the heights it stood—brown and weather-beaten, with a thick blanket of snow on the roof, and piles of snow against its wooden sides.

Franz was very tired. He wondered if anyone *would* go to the hut that night. Perhaps it would be empty, and he might have gone to the ski race after all. He might have won it, and been back at home telling Mother all about it by now.

He pushed open the hut door, and as he went in, he heard voices. He heard a man say,

"Oh, well, if there's no oil, we can't even make

ourselves a cup of coffee. Bad luck, isn't it?"

There were two men there—one fair and the other dark. In the half darkness of the hut, they saw Franz standing shyly by the door.

"Hello!" said one. "You've come to a very poor hut. There's not a drop of oil in the place. Not a drop!"

"Good gracious!" exclaimed the other. "It's only a boy! Whatever are you doing up here all alone?"

"I've brought the oil," said Franz.

In a very short time the lamp and the stove were alight, the hut was warm and cosy, and Franz and the two men were eating a fine supper and sipping hot coffee. The men were so friendly and kind, and so grateful to Franz for bringing the oil, that soon he found himself telling them all that had happened. He told them about Father being ill, and not able to come to the hut. He told them about himself, and how he wanted to be a champion skier when he grew older— champion of Austria, holder of the speed record for Europe, like Karl Engels. He told them about the ski race he had hoped to win.

"And now I've missed it," he ended sadly.

"Well, I think you're a very brave boy," said one, "and I'm proud to meet you."

"And you haven't told us your name yet," said the other. "What is it?"

"Franz."

"Mine is Julius," said the man with fair hair.

"And mine is Karl," added the dark one, leaning forward to shake hands. Franz's eyes opened wide as the lamp light shone on his new friend's face. He had seen that face before! Of course he had. He'd seen photographs of it in every paper. It was the face of the champion skier of Austria, the holder of the speed record for Europe.

"Karl?" murmured Franz in wonder.

"Karl Engels," said Karl with a smile.

* * * * * *

So Franz slept the night in the hut with Karl and Julius. Early next day they arose and had breakfast, leaving everything tidy and clean, ready for the next travellers who should pass that way. Then they closed the door, and fastened on their skis. The air was cold, for though it was nearly light, the sun had not yet risen above the mountains.

"I have to go this way," said Franz, pointing across the snow.

"We'll come with you part of the way," replied Julius. "Then when your house comes into sight, we'll branch off to the west."

"Can you spare the time?" asked Franz.

"Oh, yes," said Karl. "Besides, we want to see what your skiing is like."

Down the slope they started—Karl first, then Franz, then Julius, each keeping the same distance from the others—following Karl's tracks in a wide zig-zag pattern down the mountain side. The wind met them in a cold little rush, and their skis sent tiny fountains of powdered snow into the air.

After a while Karl stood and waited for the others to catch up with him. He watched Franz coming nearer. Down the slope came Franz. His eyes shone and his heart was full of happiness. His skis seemed to skim over the ground without effort. He seemed almost to fly. But what would Karl think of his skiing? Would he—would he think it was good?

As Franz reached the end of the slope, Karl Engels came forward with a smile of admiration on his sunburnt face.

"That was a fine bit of skiing, Franz," he said.

And at that moment the sun rose above the mountain.

The snow sparkled against a sky suddenly blue, and the mountain peaks glowed pink and gold, as one by one they were bathed in the glory of morning.

Mother Teresa

Agnes sat, spellbound, in a corner of the classroom, listening to the lady in the strange black dress. The lady was a nun and was talking to the children about life in the far off country of India, where she worked to help the poor. Agnes was twelve years old and she had never left the little town in Yugoslavia where she had been born.

The nun talked of the sadness and illness of the poor people who owned nothing but the rags they wore. She talked of the villages where the dry ground was hard and stony. She told of people who couldn't grow enough food for themselves and their children. She talked of the children with no mother or father, no home or family around them.

Agnes felt very sorry for them. She too was poor, but she had a father and mother, a brother and sister. She knew what it was to belong to a loving family. To her it seemed the saddest thing in the world that there should be people who were ill and unhappy and had no one to care for them.

Agnes decided there and then that she too would become a nun. More than anything she wanted to follow the lady in the simple black dress and go to the poor unhappy people of India. She wanted to give them what little help she could.

In the years that followed, Agnes worked hard at school. She had many friends and she loved her family. But the day came when she knew she must leave them all behind. She must become a nun and go to India to do the work she had chosen.

When she became a nun, Agnes had to change her name. The church welcomed her in and gave her the new name of Teresa.

At first Teresa was very lonely. It was not easy for her to leave the friends and family she had known and loved so long. But perhaps she felt that being alone like this helped her to understand what life was like for those who had no family or friends.

Slowly she settled down in her new country. For many years she taught in a school for girls in the large, bustling city of Calcutta. The school was a big white building, surrounded by beautiful gardens. Teresa loved teaching, and was very happy there. But often she looked over the high wall round the gardens and saw beyond it the poverty and disease of the poorest people of Calcutta. At last she could wait no longer.

She gave up her job as a teacher and wearing only the simplest and cheapest white dress, she went out among the poor.

She had no money and nowhere to live. But she went around the city streets helping the poorest beggars.

News of her work spread. People who were ill came to Teresa to beg for help. Friends from the school came to join her in her work. They were given the use of an old temple building, and there they set up their first hospital.

Teresa called it Nirmal Hriday, The Place of the Pure Heart.

She and her helpers worked day and night. Anyone who came to Nirmal Hriday was taken in. No matter how poor, ill or dirty they were, they were given shelter and food. Most of all they were given love. Teresa believed that what people need most is to have someone who really cares for them.

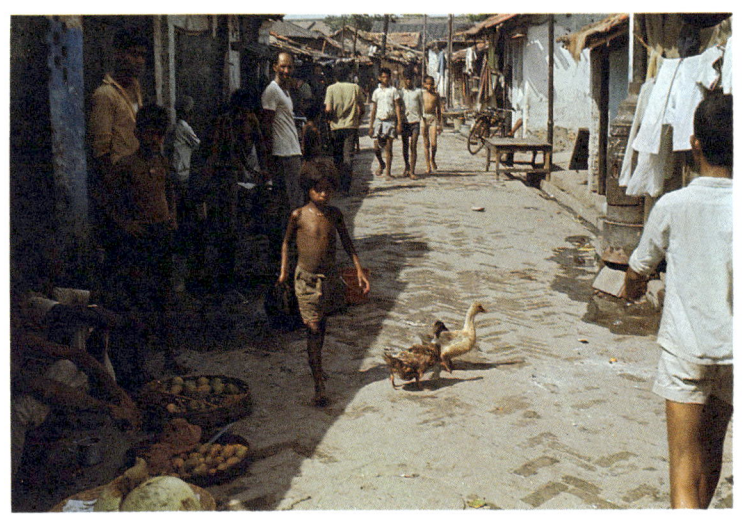

She and her friends went out into the poor streets of Calcutta, and where they found dirt and disease they gave love and kindness. Many people brought to her children who were alone. Some had no parents. Others were left by families who couldn't afford to feed them. Many children were left with Teresa because they had been born mentally or physically handicapped. None was turned away. Teresa took in all the children, and because they couldn't live in the hospital with the sick and the dying, she started a home for them.

More and more people heard of Teresa's work and came to see for themselves what she did. Many stayed to help and gave her their time and their money.

Slowly the homes and hospitals spread all over

India. Many people offered to build new hospitals and clinics for her, but Teresa always refused. She said that the poorest people would be afraid to come into a shining new building. It was for this reason too that she and her helpers always dressed in the same simple clothes, like those the peasant people wore.

Mother Teresa, as she is known, became famous not only in India but all round the world. In 1979 the Government of Sweden gave her the Nobel Peace Prize for her work. This is a prize of a medal and a large sum of money which is given each year to the person who has done most for the cause of peace in the world. Mother Teresa travelled to Stockholm in her simple dress, to accept the prize from the King and Queen of Sweden. She was very proud of the medal, but the prize did not change her in any way.

The money was used to set up more clinics, hospitals, schools and homes. Her ideas spread all over India, and wherever there are poor people, there are homes. Wherever there is disease and loneliness Mother Teresa and her helpers are to be found.

Moira Miller

Grandfather's Ship

People wondered why Don had chosen to become a deep sea diver. There were so many other things he could have been. Whatever had put such an idea into his mind?

"Who suggested it?" he was asked.

"No one," Don always replied. But though no one had actually mentioned deep sea diving to him, it was a story that his grandfather had told him long ago that had first given him the idea.

Don had been a little boy then, staying in Grandfather's white cottage that stood high on the cliffs, overlooking the sea. It happened like this.

Grandfather sat in the window seat, puffing at his pipe, and watching the distant curls of foam on the sea.

"It must be nice to watch the sea every day," said Don, sitting down beside him.

"I've watched the sea every day of my life," replied Grandfather, slowly.

"Even when you were a boy?" asked Don, hoping he might get the old man to tell him a story.

"Yes. As long as I can remember I've slept in the room above, with my bed close to the window facing the sea."

"Ships don't often pass this way, do they?"

"No. It's a lonely bit of coast."

Grandfather's eyes gleamed suddenly at a memory, and he leaned forward and said in a hushed voice,

"Once I saw—"

Then he stopped.

"What did you see?" asked Don.

"Oh, nothing," murmured Grandfather.

"Tell me," urged Don.

"What's the good?" said Grandfather. "I've told dozens of people, and no one has ever believed me."

"Please tell me."

Don looked so anxious and excited that Grandfather could not say no to him. So the story was told, and all the time streaks of white foam curled backwards and forwards on the distant sea.

"One night long ago," said Grandfather, "there was a terrible storm. The wind rattled the doors as if it would shake the cottage to pieces, and even from this distance I could hear the angry roar of the sea. I was very small, and hadn't even learnt to speak properly. I sat up in bed and looked out into the darkness. At the other side of the room my brother went on sleeping. I remember hearing a loud crack, as the wind tore a branch from the apple tree in the garden, and then—then—"

"Yes?" whispered Don.

"There was a flash of lightning. It seemed to split the sky in two. And in that moment of light I saw a ship go down. So great and beautiful she was, with her masts pointing to the sky, and all her sails setting like folded shadows. So beautiful—and she was gone."

"Oh!" murmured Don, and it seemed to him that he could hear the storm, and see the ship sinking.

"In the morning," continued Grandfather, "my

mother was sad to see the apple tree broken, and my father had to mend the gate, which the wind had damaged. I tried to tell them about the ship, but they didn't understand. They only said, 'Go and play, Martin,' and went on talking about the gate and the apple tree."

"And didn't they ever understand?" asked Don.

"Yes. Years later when I could explain, I told them again. They said I had dreamt it. They said that if a ship had really gone down, someone else would have seen it too, or at least heard of it. My brother teased me about dreaming, and after that, if anything sounded impossible, the family always laughed and said, 'Like Martin's ship.' They've said that all through the years. People still say it, only now they say 'Grandfather's ship' instead."

Grandfather moved in his chair, and sighed.

"No one believes me," he added.

"I do!" exclaimed Don. "I believe you."

He stared out at the sea for a long while, his eyes shining, and his mind full of the story.

"Such a beautiful ship she was," said Grandfather again, "such a beautiful ship."

And then the idea had come to Don, that when he

grew up, he would become a deep sea diver, and one day he would dive into that same stretch of sea, and find Grandfather's ship for him.

So here he was, grown up, and trained as a deep sea diver, and here he was in a rowing boat with his friend Derek, in the very stretch of sea where Grandfather's ship had gone down.

"This is the place," said Don, bringing the boat to a standstill.

"Lovely calm day," murmured Derek. "I say," he added. "Don't be disappointed if you don't find anything, will you? I mean, your grandfather *might* have dreamt it or imagined it."

"Yes, he might," replied Don, "but he still believes that he saw the ship, and somehow I've always believed it too." He pulled on three pairs of thick socks, and put three woollen jerseys on over his clothes. It was hot up here in the sun, but he knew it would be cold at the bottom of the sea. He fastened pads on his shoulders, and then put on his rubber diving suit, and boots with lead soles.

"Good luck!" said Derek, and he slipped the helmet over Don's head, and screwed it firmly in place. Don climbed on to the ladder leading from the boat down into the water. He waited while Derek arranged the air pipe by which he was to breathe, and the lead weights which were to help him to sink to the bottom. Derek started the air pump. Don waved his hand, climbed down the ladder, and slid down the rope hanging beneath.

In a few seconds he was standing at the bottom of the sea. At first he saw nothing but sand beneath his feet, misty grey sea water all around, and a few startled fish swimming away. Then he saw twisting strands of seaweed, and strange sea creatures of red and pink.

But he couldn't see a ship. He walked about on the floor of the ocean, looking through the glass window of his helmet, searching everywhere.

Perhaps Grandfather's ship had been a dream after all, or perhaps already the sand had buried it for ever. On and on went Don, but it was no good. Wherever he went, there were only coloured fish and straggling seaweeds.

Sadly he walked back, and pulled at the life line, to show Derek that he was coming up again. Don knew that it was dangerous for a diver to stay down too long, and also that it was dangerous to rise to the surface too quickly. As he went higher and higher he rested several times on the rope. Then at last he came to the ladder, and Derek helped him carefully into the boat.

As soon as Don's helmet was off, Derek asked, "Did you find the ship?"

Wearily Don shook his head. When he had rested a while, and become used to breathing fresh air again, he said,

"Let's row further out, and try again."

"All right," agreed Derek, taking the oars.

So once more, in even deeper water, Don went down to the bottom of the sea. As before, he saw nothing at first except sand and misty grey sea water. Then he saw gaily-coloured sea creatures and strands of curly seaweed—and rocks a little way ahead.

"I guess Grandfather did dream it after all," he thought. He walked round the rocks, moving carefully so that his air pipe should not get tangled. And there before him was a great shadow. Could it be? He hardly dared to hope. He remembered Grandfather saying,

"So beautiful she was, with her masts pointing to the sky, and all her sails setting like folded shadows."

Oh, if Grandfather could only see what Don was seeing now!

There stood the ship half buried in the sand, with shell fish and seaweed clinging to her sides, and black and scarlet fish swimming across her decks. The masts and the sails had been broken and washed away. There were gaping cracks and broken doors where cabins had once been, and huge holes where the wood was rotting. Slowly the ship was breaking up, there at the bottom of the sea—but oh, she was beautiful still!

"I must take something for Grandfather," thought Don, "even if it's only a bit of wood."

He looked round, and climbed in and out among the wreckage. She was a foreign ship, he could tell, and he wondered from which country she had sailed so bravely in the days when Grandfather had been a little boy.

There was one cabin Don could not enter, for the door still hung firmly in place, and was wedged so tightly that it would not open. He leaned his shoulder against it, and pushed with all his strength.

The door burst open suddenly, and Don stumbled inside, almost falling against a small iron box in the corner.

"What's this?" he said to himself, stooping to lift the box. At that moment he felt a tug at his life line. That was Derek saying,

"Time to come up."

Oh, he must just peep in this old box first! Quickly he pulled open the rusty lid—and there inside were coins—golden coins! Another tug came at the life line.

"You've been under long enough. You must come up at once," Derek was trying to say.

But here were golden coins, hundreds and hundreds of them—treasure from a foreign land!

"This is something to take to Grandfather!" said Don aloud, and clinging to the box, he climbed out of the cabin, and started going up and up through the misty grey water, leaving the ship alone and beautiful, like a shadow on the floor of the sea.

Eros

Piccadilly Circus is the name of a place in the centre of London where many streets meet. In the middle of Piccadilly there is a small island of stone, and on this island there is a statue called Eros. Eros holds a bow and arrow, and leans forward as if he is flying over London. On the steps below him women used to sit with baskets of violets and snowdrops, or bunches of pink carnations and tight little rosebuds.

All around are buses and lorries, and taxis and cars coming from north and south and east and west. Day and night the busy London traffic swirls round the small, stone island, and day after day people hurry past on their way to shops and theatres and stations and offices.

Everyone knows Eros. Taxi drivers look up at him, and say,

"Ah, Eros! Here we are at Piccadilly!"

Children, holding tightly to their mothers' hands as they cross the road, try to catch a glimpse of him between the rows of traffic. But no one seems to have time to go up the steps, and read the words that are written below the statue. And many people, though they know Eros so well, don't know at all why he is there.

He is there to remind them of a story about a man called the Earl of Shaftesbury, who spent his whole life helping children.

In those days it was no fun to be a child. Most children, unless they were rich, had no time to play, and very little time even to sleep.

They worked in factories and mills from early in the morning till late at night. They worked on farms and in brickyards. They climbed up chimneys to sweep away soot. They crawled down mines to push along trucks of coal. These children did not know what it was like to be clean, well fed and happy.

The Earl of Shaftesbury was rich, yet when he was a child, he was unhappy too. His father was always busy, and his mother was interested only in going to parties and wearing beautiful clothes. Even the servants sometimes forgot about him. So the little boy was often lonely in his big house, and sad because it seemed as if no one cared for him.

Perhaps that was why, when he grew up, he cared so much and worked so hard for unhappy children.

At first he wondered what he could do to help them.

He hadn't enough money to feed all the hungry ones, or to take all the ill ones away from the work that tired them, but there was something he could do. He could go into Parliament, and try to make Parliament pass laws to help the children of England.

He started with the children in factories and mills, where wool, silk and cotton cloth were made. He visited one factory after another, watching and talking to poor girls and boys of six and seven, and even four and five years of age, who worked the machines. They had to get up at three in the morning, while it was dark and they were still half asleep, and they had to work till ten o'clock at night. The Earl of Shaftesbury noticed how thin and pale they were, and he knew that though they were hungry, they were usually too tired even to eat.

For a long while he worked hard, writing and making speeches, and at last Parliament listened to him, and passed a law saying that no children were to work in factories.

Then he looked round for other unhappy children, and he decided to help those who worked in coal mines. The underground passages in mines were very narrow, so the tiniest children were sent to crawl along them, pulling the trucks of coal. These children hardly ever saw sunshine and blue skies. They were always in the dark, with not even enough space for growing properly, but soon the Earl of Shaftesbury's work set them free too.

Now there were chimney sweep boys who needed his help. Chimneys were wide in those days, and small boys were made to climb up inside them, to clean them. Many were the nights in which the Earl of Shaftesbury lay awake thinking about them. He wrote letters to the papers, and made speeches in Parliament, until a law was made to save these children too.

After that, he helped children who worked on farms and in brickyards, and he built schools and homes for them.

In London he found hundreds of children who just wandered about the streets, because they had no one to look after them. They had no homes to shelter them, so at night they slept in doorways and under arches. He had a big ship sent to the River Thames, and there the homeless children were able to live, with good food to eat, clean beds to sleep in, and kind people to look after them.

There was no end to the kindness of the Earl of

Shaftesbury. Year by year he worked, until, by the time he was an old man, there were hardly any unhappy children left in England.

When he died, money was collected for a statue by which to remember him. The people who gave the money were the children whom he had helped. They were grown up by then, but they remembered how this great man had saved them from heavy work as young children in factories and on farms, in mines and mills, and brickyards and chimneys, and they remembered how he had given them freedom and happiness.

And the statue that was set up in his memory was the statue of Eros on the small stone island in Piccadilly Circus in the centre of London.

The Seventh Climb

Tenzing Norgay was one of the Sherpa people who live in the high valleys of Nepal, a country to the north of India. The Sherpas do not read or write so there was no way of knowing exactly when Tenzing's birthday was. It would not have mattered anyhow, as Sherpas do not celebrate their birthdays.

Tenzing was one of a large family, and grew up in a hill village. The family lived upstairs in a white stone house with a roof made of wooden tiles. Downstairs they kept their animals. Like the rest of the villagers they had little money, but they were very happy.

As Tenzing grew up, it was his job to go with his brothers and look after the herd of yaks that the family owned. The yak is a very important animal to the Sherpas. It gives them milk from which they make butter and cheese. They make clothes and shoes from the wool and hide, and they use the dried dung as fuel for their fires. Tenzing and his brothers spent long days climbing on the high mountains around the village, following their herd of yaks.

Tenzing always loved the mountains. He had been born near Mount Everest, the highest mountain in the world. For the Sherpa people Mount Everest is a special mountain. They call it Chomolungma—the mountain so high no bird can fly over it. (It is in the middle of the picture opposite.) As a little boy Tenzing would sit and gaze up at the mountain and dream. He knew that nobody had ever climbed to the top. He was determined that one day he would do it.

As he grew up he longed to leave the village. He had heard of other Sherpas who had gone into India and because they were fine climbers they were hired by teams who came from far countries to climb the high mountains around Everest. Sometimes the Sherpas came back to the village wearing strange clothes and telling stories of their adventures. One of the men allowed Tenzing to try on his climbing boots, but they were so big that Tenzing couldn't walk in them! He listened to the stories and made up his mind that one day he would leave the village and go back with the men to India.

The day came at last when he was about eighteen. A group of young men from the village were leaving to find work in the town of Darjeeling in India. Tenzing took some food and a blanket and went with them. For many days they travelled across wild running rivers, through high mountain passes, down into the jungle of the foothills until at last they came to Darjeeling.

At first it was difficult for Tenzing to find work. Nobody wanted to take him as a climber because he was too young. So he took a job looking after a herd of cows for a farmer. Gradually he learned the Nepali language and he dressed in Nepali clothes. The next time he tried to join a team of climbers they wouldn't take him because they thought he was a Nepali! "You dress and speak like a Nepali," they said. "We are looking only for Sherpas. They are the finest climbers."

At last his chance came. In 1935, he joined a British team led by a famous climber called Eric Shipton. As luck would have it, the mountain they set out to climb was Everest!

It was then that Tenzing found he was different from the other Sherpas. Shipton decided that they wouldn't be able to climb right to the top of the mountain, but he set out to go as high as he could. As they climbed higher and higher, the air became thinner and thinner. But where the others found it difficult to breathe in the thin air, Tenzing climbed on easily. He found that the higher he climbed the fitter he felt.

When at last Shipton turned back, the other Sherpas went down willingly. But Tenzing longed to go on to the top, and he hated climbing down the mountain again.

He made many more attempts on Everest over the years. He climbed with Indian, German, French and British teams. Time and again he set out hoping that this would be the best climb. Perhaps this would be the team that would take him to the top of the great Chomolungma. He came very close on his sixth attempt, climbing with a Swiss team in 1952. He and the leader of the team pitched the highest camp men had made on the mountain, but in the end they were driven back by the cruel icy weather. Everest had beaten him again.

After that Tenzing became ill and he returned to Darjeeling. For many months he rested. He was married by this time and had a family of his own. His wife was happy to have him safely home again, but just as he seemed to be settling down to a quiet life there came word of another climb. A British team, led by Colonel John Hunt, were coming to India in the spring of 1953. They were determined that this time they would climb Everest.

Tenzing went into training. He spent days and weeks walking in the mountains around Darjeeling with a pack full of stones on his back. He worked hard, and by the time the team came to Darjeeling looking for Sherpas, Tenzing was ready to go with them.

His wife was not too pleased, but one of his daughters, who was still at school, was very happy. Before he left she gave him the only thing she had to give. It was a little stub of red and blue pencil.

"Put it in the right place," she said, and Tenzing

knew just where that place was.

It was decided that there should be two teams ready to climb to the top. If one failed, the other would be ready to take over. Evans and Bourdillon were chosen as one team. Tenzing, along with a climber from New Zealand called Edmund Hillary were the other team. At the beginning these four climbed together, getting to know each other. Higher and higher they climbed, taking equipment and tents up the mountain. At last, after three weeks, they set up Camp Eight. From there they were within sight of the summit.

The men were tired and cold. In the thin air they were unable to sleep without pills, and they didn't want to eat. They were always thirsty, though, and a favourite drink was powdered lemon juice and sugar mixed with hot water. They drank so much of it that Tenzing said they should be known as the "Lemon-juice Expedition"!

It was decided that Evans and Bourdillon should try first for the top. Colonel Hunt and one of the Sherpas climbed on ahead and set up Camp Nine, high on the icy windswept slopes. Evans and Bourdillon set out on the 23rd of May. They picked up the extra oxygen tanks that had been left at Camp Nine, but like Tenzing the year before, they were unable to go on. They knew that if they did they would probably die on the mountain. Sadly they turned back, leaving as much oxygen as they could for Tenzing and Hillary, who would follow them. By the time they reached Camp Eight again, Bourdillon was very ill.

The team lay in their tents that night as a fierce storm screamed across the mountain-side. Tenzing knew now that the next attempt on the top must be his and Hillary's. Through that last night he lay remembering the men who had died on the mountain. He thought of his home and family far below. He thought of the next day and the final climb, and at last he fell asleep.

Early the next morning the wind had dropped. It seemed that the climb must be now or never. Tenzing and Hillary set off from Camp Nine. They found the oxygen tanks the others had left and they struggled on up until at last they came to a sheltered spot that Tenzing had seen from below the year before. He had thought then that it would be a good place to make the last camp before the top. He and Hillary chopped away

Tenzing (on the right) and Hillary, photographed on the way to Camp Nine.

the ice to make a space to pitch the one tiny tent they had carried up with them. Through the night the icy wind whistled around them. They lay huddled together, holding down the sides of the tent.

At dawn the next day they crawled out of the tent into a wonderfully still and clear morning. Above them the sky was a deep clear blue. The dazzling white summit of the mountain blinded them in the brilliant sunlight. Scattered down the mountain were the tiny clusters of tents. Down there were the men who had helped them to reach the top. Far beneath, in the clear air,

Tenzing could see the holy place where he had been born.

Slowly and carefully they edged out across the snow face. One wrong step here and the snow would crumble, tumbling them thousands of metres down the mountainside. They edged across, slowly, roped together, reaching for hand and foot holds in the snow. They climbed at last off the snow on to a firm rocky ridge that led to the top, and they stopped to breathe again.

Tenzing picked up two small stones and put them in his pocket, and then together he and Hillary climbed the last few metres to the top.

At last they had succeeded. After long months of looking and climbing always upwards they stood together at the top! The impossible dream had come true. They could climb no higher. They shook hands and thumped each other on the back until they were gasping for breath. Hillary pulled his camera from inside his anorak where he had kept it safe and warm and he took a picture of Tenzing.

In the photograph Tenzing is standing on the summit holding an ice axe. Round the handle are wound the flags of the United Nations, Britain, India and Nepal. He left the flags on the summit.

There was something else he left with them. He scraped a hole in the snow and buried the little red and blue pencil stub that his daughter had given him. Because in his country a gift of sweets is a special thing to give to someone you love, he left a few sweets beside it.

"Thuji chey, Chomolungma," he said. "I am grateful, Chomolungma."

The mountain he loved had finally allowed him to reach the top.

Fifteen minutes later Tenzing and Hillary set off for the bottom again.

* * * * * *

The story of the climb first appeared in newspapers all round the world on the morning of the second of June, 1953. It was the day of Queen Elizabeth II's coronation.

Tenzing Norgay had left Darjeeling on the first of March as a quiet unknown family man from a simple peasant home. By the time he returned to that home his face and his name were famous everywhere.

Moira Miller

When Anna Danced

The theatre was full. In a few moments the chattering would stop, and the lights would be dimmed. In a few moments the curtains would part, and the ballet would begin.

Anna dangled her thin legs, and looked round in wonder at all the people—so many people. Some of them wore beautiful clothes and shining jewels. Anna's mother had no beautiful clothes or shining jewels, for she was poor and had to work hard to buy even enough food to eat. Anna moved a little closer to her.

"When I grow up," she thought, "I'll earn a lot of money, so that I can buy pretty dresses and warm fur coats for Mother." She wondered what she would be when she grew older. Perhaps she would be an artist, for she liked drawing. Then she could buy a big house, and Mother wouldn't have to work any more. Their own house was so small, and Mother was always worrying about things they needed but couldn't afford to buy, and about clothes that wore out too quickly.

At that moment the curtains moved just the tiniest bit, and all the long velvet folds shivered as if a breeze were passing by. Quickly Anna looked in front of her.

She didn't want to miss anything. But the curtain was still again, and nothing happened after all.

"I wonder if it's still snowing outside," whispered Anna. Mother smiled.

"It's nice and warm in here," she said.

"When will the curtains open, Mother?"

"Very soon, now."

"What is the ballet called, Mother?"

"The Sleeping Beauty."

The Sleeping Beauty. That was a story Anna had always loved. How interesting it would be to see it acted and danced upon a stage.

Anna was eight years old, and this was the first time she had ever been to a theatre. Mother had saved and saved to buy the tickets. It was a special treat.

There was music. The curtains shivered again. Slowly they parted. Slowly they opened. Anna's eyes opened too—wide and wondering, for she saw a room in a royal palace, and a baby princess lying in a golden cradle. Watching over the baby were nurses in pink, and nurses in blue, who pulled a golden cord to rock the cradle to and fro. Down the steps and into the room came the King and Queen, and all the people who had come to see the baby. There were noblemen in velvet suits of black and crimson. There were ladies in silk and satin.

Then came the fairies, each with a present and a wish for the little princess. The Lilac Fairy came, and the Fairy of the Pine Woods, the Cherry Blossom Fairy, and the Fairy of the Song Birds. One gave the baby the gift of dancing, and one the gift of music. One gave her the gift of beauty, and one the gift of song.

"Just like the story," thought Anna. She wanted to whisper, "Isn't it lovely?" to her mother, but she could not turn her eyes away from the stage even for a second, for now the fairies were dancing.

The Fairy of the Pine Woods danced slowly and gracefully to soft, sleepy music. The Cherry Blossom Fairy jumped and whirled faster and faster. The Fairy of the Song Birds gave a quick little fluttering dance, but the Lilac Fairy's dance was the best of all. Her feet moved like magic to the gay, silvery music. She jumped and spun and turned in the air. She stepped and ran, and twirled on her toes.

"How wonderful," thought Anna. "How wonderful!"

She forgot that she was a poor little girl in a shabby dress. She thought that she was the Lilac Fairy dancing up there on the stage—pointing her toes and fluttering her arms, and dancing and dancing in delight.

So the ballet went on, telling the old story that Anna knew so well, of how the princess grew up and pricked her finger, and fell asleep, and how the prince came to waken her.

Anna leaned forward, noticing every detail and every step of the dancing—listening to every note of the music. Oh, it was wonderful! It was like a dream—a long, perfect dream. How well the princess danced! Oh, to dance like that! It seemed to Anna now, that she was the princess, rising on her toes, spreading wide her arms—jumping, whirling, dancing and dancing.

Suddenly the ballet was over and the curtains closed, hanging again in long velvet folds. The lights went up, and people put on their coats and cloaks, and began chattering, and walking to the doors.

Anna's eyes were like stars, and her thoughts were still with "The Sleeping Beauty". She didn't hear when her mother spoke to her, and when they went into the street, she scarcely felt the cold wind and the snowflakes that whirled in her face.

Mother held her hand tightly, and hurried her away from the theatre. This was the land of Russia, and there were horses pulling sleighs along the wide streets. The sound of muffled footsteps mingled with the music of sleigh bells over the white snow. But the music ringing in Anna's ears was the music of the ballet. She said not a word. She only held her mother's hand, and hurried along beside her.

"She must be tired," thought Mother.

Soon they reached the narrow street where they lived, and came to their own small house. Mother opened the door, and held it for Anna to go through. But Anna stood silent a moment on the dark pavement, with the cold wind tugging at her shabby coat, and the

snow blowing round her.

"Mother," she said, "I know now what I'm going to be when I grow up! I'm going to be a dancer."

"Are you, dear?" replied Mother, and she smiled, for she knew that little girls of eight changed their minds a dozen times before they grew up.

But Anna did not change her mind. She wanted to be a dancer, and she seemed to think of nothing else at all. Day by day she danced round the table, and in and out among the chairs—standing on her toes and holding up her thin arms, jumping and whirling, twisting and turning. She knelt on the floor, and rose slowly upwards like a flower opening. She fluttered her hands and leapt into the air like a bird flying. Oh, it was lovely to dance! Even at night in her dreams she danced—light airy dances to gay, silvery music.

At first her mother tried to make her think of other things.

"Dancing isn't all fun and beauty," she said. "It is hard work."

"But it makes me so happy, Mother."

"Dancers have to practise and practise the same steps over and over again."

"I don't mind how hard I have to work, and how

long I have to practise, if only I can be a dancer."

Mother watched Anna sometimes as she flitted round the room. There seemed something magic about her. Her feet touched the floor so lightly. Her hands moved so gracefully. She was hardly like a real little girl. She was more like a cloud drifting across the sky, or a leaf blown in the wind. And Mother knew then that Anna would never change her mind. She would always want to be a dancer. Perhaps she was born to dance.

In Russia there was a school for ballet dancers. It took children when they were ten years old, and kept them till they were sixteen. There were always hundreds and hundreds of children who wanted to go to it, but first they had tests to pass—tests in writing and arithmetic, tests in walking and moving; and only a very few children were chosen each year.

Mother explained this to Anna, and told her that if she wanted to go to the School of Dancing, she must work hard at lessons she did not like, as well as those she did like. Then when she was ten years old, she could take the tests.

"Oh, yes!" cried Anna in delight. "I *will* work hard. I'll do anything to be a dancer!"

So at ten years of age she passed into the School of Dancing. It meant leaving her mother, for it was a boarding school, and visitors were allowed only once a fortnight. At first she felt lonely and sad and shy, and she found that what Mother had said was true. Dancing was *not* all fun and beauty. It was hard work. Besides learning ordinary school lessons, she had to do exercises, and the same steps over and over again, until she was so tired that she could hardly stand.

But she soon began to get used to it, and she soon made friends with other children. When they asked her name, she answered, "Anna Pavlova," and to herself she thought, "One day everyone in Russia will know my name, for one day I'll be a great dancer."

She practised and practised, and when other children went out to play or to rest, she stayed behind and practised again. Teachers and famous dancers who watched her said to each other,

"There's magic about Anna Pavlova. Surely she was born to dance!"

So the little girl Anna grew up, and all her dreams came true. She became a ballet dancer, dancing in the very theatre at which she had seen "The Sleeping Beauty" so long ago.

Everyone in Russia knew her name. She was famous. People came in crowds to watch her dance. Mother did not have to work any more. Anna bought her a beautiful house with servants; and pretty dresses and warm fur coats and shining jewels. Anna danced and danced. She was as graceful as grasses swaying in the breeze. She was as light as thistledown. She was happy because she danced.

Then one day she decided to leave Russia and dance in other countries.

"Don't go away," begged her friends. "Russians love to see ballet, but people in other countries know nothing about it. They may not like it."

"I'll teach them to like it," replied Anna.

Soon the whole world was ringing with her name. Wherever she went, people flocked to see her. They crowded into theatres and halls to watch her dance. They sent flowers to her—flowers of all kinds and colours and perfumes. They waited hours in the streets just to watch her pass.

One day as Anna left a theatre, a woman ran out from the crowd, with a baby in her arms.

"Please—I want you to touch my baby," she said. Anna smiled, and held the baby for a moment. The baby, of course, was too small to understand, but as Anna saw the joy in the mother's face, she suddenly understood how much happiness her dancing gave to people. Before this, she had danced because she loved to dance—because it made her happy. Now, she danced also because people loved to watch her—and because it made them happy.

So she went on dancing, in great theatres and tiny halls, to kings and queens, to rich and poor. She danced in England and France and Germany, in America, India, Japan. On and on through the world she danced. There was magic in her steps. She was so light, so airy, like a cloud drifting across the sky, like a leaf blown in the wind. And the world was happy when Anna Pavlova danced.

Reynard

In the middle of Hazel Wood, in a small patch of grass, grew a great oak tree. Its twisted roots sheltered many wild creatures, and there in a deep burrow lived a mother fox and her three cubs. The babies were pretty little things, just like balls of yellow-red fluff, with sharp faces and bright eyes; and they rolled and romped like puppies.

One night when they were only a few weeks old, their mother went out hunting, and didn't come back. The cubs didn't know what had happened to her, and for several days they lay in the burrow, crying and calling, until they were weak with hunger. One of them, a little braver than the others, began to drag himself slowly up the tunnel towards the daylight.

Soon after, a farmer passed that way, and noticed what he thought was a little bundle of brown fur lying on the grass. How surprised he was to find that it was a little fox cub! He picked him up, and took him home. His children were delighted, and wanted to play with the little fox, but the farmer took him to the barn where his dog was lying with her puppies. He made room for the cub, and put him to feed with the others. The mother dog didn't mind, and soon the cub was sleeping among his new brothers and sisters.

The next morning when the children went to look at their new pet, they could see that he was feeling better, and they talked a great deal about whose pet he should be. But their father settled it by saying that as one had some rabbits, and another had some bantam fowls, the baby fox should belong to Kitty, who, you may be sure, was delighted.

At school she had been reading a story about a fox called Reynard, so she said that this would be a good name for him.

She brought her friends to see him, and they all liked her strange pet.

Reynard grew until he was no longer a fluffy ball of fur, but a handsome fox with a long nose, bright eyes, and a bushy tail with a white tip. He loved to play games with his dog brothers and sisters, and to growl and snap as they romped together in the garden. He soon learnt to answer to his name, but only when Kitty called him.

One day Kitty decided to take him for a walk in the village. She found an old dog collar and lead, and after some trouble she managed to get the collar round

Reynard's neck. Off she went, feeling very proud with her fox trotting by her side. She met some friends in the village, and she stopped so that they could see Reynard. But Reynard didn't like all these strangers, and he shrank close against her legs, trying to hide himself.

Kitty bent down to pick him up, but the lead slipped out of her hand, and Reynard was off down the road like a flash, running towards home. She called and called him, but he took no notice, and she had to run after him.

When she reached home, she found him crouching in

the farthest and darkest corner of the barn. As she was alone, he was willing to come to her, but as she patted him, she could feel him trembling.

Reynard grew braver as he grew older, and as foxes are sensible animals, he soon learnt that not all strange things are dangerous. Later he could often be seen walking in the village with Kitty, quite unafraid so long as she was near.

And then one night the trouble began. A hen disappeared. Next morning there were feathers in the henhouse and outside on the ground to show what had happened. There were still more feathers and well-picked bones in the barn where Reynard slept at night.

"Oh, Reynard," Kitty cried, "how could you kill the chicken? Whatever will Dad say?"

But Reynard looked back at her without understanding. He didn't know what all the fuss was about. It was in his nature to hunt for food and he couldn't help killing fowls, though he was clever enough to sense that Kitty was angry and upset.

"What's all this?" said her father, frowning over the feathers. "Well, that decides it, Kitty. I'm sorry, but you can't keep your pet any longer. You can't make a wild animal into a tame one. I've had complaints about missing hens from the neighbours lately, and I began to think that Reynard was the cause."

"Give him one more chance, Dad," cried Kitty.

"No, it wouldn't be fair to Reynard," Dad answered. "You would have to shut him up at nights, just when he was longing to be out hunting like other foxes. He'll fret and become unhappy. You can't treat him like a dog. As it is, I'll have to be very careful of my hens."

"Then what must I do, Dad?" Kitty asked.

"You must let him go. Take him back into the country," her father answered. "You remember the place I once showed you, where I noticed a family of cubs? Well, leave him there. He'll soon meet a fox family."

Kitty obeyed with a heavy heart. She found the old dog collar once more, and in the cool of the evening she led Reynard into the country. She stopped in a place where there were thick bushes, and stooped down to take off his collar.

"I'm so sorry, Reynard," she said. "I wish you could stay. I'll be lonely without you." She patted his handsome back, and then turned quickly and went home as fast as she could.

She half hoped that Reynard would follow her, or come back to the barn at nightfall, but Reynard behaved like the fox he was. He was free. Being a wild animal, he didn't even stop to watch Kitty go, as a dog would have done, but he trotted off quickly into the bushes to look for fox friends. He had learnt much about humans from living among them, and he was not at all puzzled because Kitty had left him. He soon found a family of foxes, and was quite happy.

As for Kitty, she went home through the fields, still hoping that Reynard would slip back to the farm. When she reached the house, however, her father met her. He knew she would miss her fox, so he held out a little puppy to her.

"This is for you, Kitty," he said kindly. "I thought you'd like a new pet. Take care of it."

"Thank you, Dad," she said. "Isn't he lovely?" She took the warm little puppy in her arms, and she soon forgot to look for Reynard's return.

Of course Reynard never went back. Though Kitty knew he was happier in his new home, and she no longer wanted him back, she still used to look for him sometimes when she walked in the fields.

Adapted

The Boy Who Liked Music

Nanerl was learning to play the clavier. The clavier was like a piano, only smaller. She sat up straight on the stool to do her practising. Her legs dangled, and didn't nearly reach the floor, for she was only eight years old. She pressed down the little white keys with her fingers, just as the music book showed her. The soft, gay little tune she played went lilting through the house. In another room her three-year-old brother Wolfgang was playing with his toys. He heard the music, and sat still for a moment, listening. Then he jumped up from the floor, and ran into the room where the clavier was.

He held out his arms to Nanerl, and she lifted him on to her lap, and went on playing as well as she could.

"Let me try," said Wolfgang.

"All right," laughed Nanerl.

Wolfgang was only three, and she thought he would just bang notes anywhere, and make a jangling noise, but he didn't. He put two fingers carefully on two notes, leaving out one in between. It made quite a pleasant sound. He did it again with two more notes, leaving out one in between.

"I can make music," he said happily, and he went

all the way up the clavier, and all the way down again, playing chords with his baby fingers.

After that, he took a great interest in Nanerl's music lessons, and he surprised everyone by remembering little pieces from her music book, and playing them himself.

"I want to learn music," he said. He said it so many times that his father began teaching him in fun. Wolfgang learnt very quickly, and could soon play a number of pieces perfectly. When he was four years old, he started making up his own tunes and playing them on the clavier. His mother and father were amazed.

"Wolfgang is a wonder child!" they said.

By the time Nanerl was eleven and Wolfgang was six, they could play the clavier so well that their father decided to show his two clever children to the world. He took them to the great cities of Europe—first to Munich, and then to Vienna.

In Vienna a message came from the Empress, asking the children to go to the palace and play to her. How excited they were! Their mother dressed them in their finest clothes, and brushed their hair till it shone. Nanerl wore a white silk frock, and Wolfgang wore a suit trimmed with broad, gold braid. They arrived at the palace, where the Empress welcomed them kindly.

You might think that a little boy of six would feel shy, playing to such a grand lady in such a fine palace, but Wolfgang didn't mind at all. He played the clavier for a while, and then he jumped on to the Empress's lap, flung his arms round her neck, and kissed her. She was delighted with the friendly little boy and his gentle sister.

After that, the names of Wolfgang Mozart and his sister Nanerl were heard all over Europe. Everyone wanted to see these wonderful children. Everyone wanted to hear them play.

The children travelled more and more, to Germany,

Austria, France, Holland and England. They must often have been tired, and sometimes they became ill, and had to rest. Then, as soon as they were better, on they would go again, playing in halls, houses, churches, making people happy to hear them, filling the world with music. And year after year as they journeyed, little Wolfgang made up tunes, hummed them in his head, wrote them down on scraps of paper and tried them on his clavier. He made tunes when he was a little boy and he went on making them all his life.

All this happened a long while ago, but the music of Wolfgang Mozart is known and remembered today. Claviers are almost forgotten, but wherever there are pianos, violins and orchestras, his music is played. So his tunes go on lilting through the world—sad tunes, solemn tunes, gay tunes, happy tunes—on and on for ever.

Star Patterns

The stars in the sky are arranged in certain patterns. Each pattern is not always in the same place. It may be the right way up in spring, and the wrong way up in autumn. It may be at the back of your house in summer, and at the front of your house in winter. But the pattern itself doesn't change, and once you know it, you will be able to find it wherever it is.

Here are three easy ones to learn. Draw them so that you remember them. Then look for them next time you are out at night when the sky is clear and the stars are shining.

Cassiopeia

Cassiopeia is easy, because it is like a large W.

The Plough

This is like a plough with a long curved handle.

Orion

Orion was supposed to be a giant. He has one star for his head, one for each shoulder, three for his belt, three for his sword hanging down, and one for each knee.

The Jar of Olives

Once upon a time there was a man named Ali, who wished to go on a journey. As he expected to be away a long time, he sold his house and his furniture, but he couldn't decide what to do with his money. He had saved a thousand pieces of gold, and he wanted to leave them in a safe place until his return.

After a while, an idea came to him. He put the gold into a large jar, and then filled the upper part of the jar with olives, so that the gold was hidden. He closed the top of the jar, and then carried it to a friend of his who was a merchant.

"Will you do something for me?" he asked. "I'm going away, as you know. Will you look after this jar of olives till I come back?"

"Certainly," replied the merchant. "Take it to my storeroom and put it where you like, and you'll find it in the same place when you return."

Ali took the jar to the storeroom, thanked his friend for his kindness, and then started on his journey. He visited one country, and then another, travelling far and wide across the world.

At last when seven years had passed, he decided to return to the town where he had lived before.

Now all this time, the jar of olives stood in the storehouse where he had left it. His friend the merchant scarcely thought of it at all, and for many years he even forgot about Ali. Then one night at supper, the merchant's wife began to talk of olives.

"I haven't tasted olives for a long while," she remarked.

"That reminds me," said the merchant. "There's a jar of olives in the storeroom. It belongs to Ali. What a long time he has been away! It must be seven years at least. Surely he'll never come back now. We may as well eat the olives if they're still good."

He stood up, taking a plate in one hand and a candle in the other.

"Oh, I don't think we ought to touch them," said his wife. "Ali trusted you with the jar. What will he think if he does return, and finds that you've opened it? Besides, the olives must be bad by now."

The merchant knew that his wife was right, but he would not listen to her. He went to the storeroom, and opened the jar. By the light of the candle, he saw at once that the olives had gone bad.

"I wonder if they're *all* bad," he thought, and he tipped the jar on its side to see. As some of the olives tumbled out, there was a rattling sound, and there upon the floor fell several pieces of gold.

"Oh!" exclaimed the merchant in delight, for he was a greedy man. Then as he looked into the jar again, he found that the lower half was filled with gold, and the olives had been put in only to hide it.

Not knowing quite what to do, he put the olives back on top of the gold, covered the jar, and went back to his wife.

"You were right," he said. "The olives were bad, so I've left them as they were."

"It's a pity you touched them," she answered. "It's wrong to touch things belonging to other people."

That night the merchant hardly slept. He wanted to take Ali's gold.

"But how can I do it so that Ali will not find out even if he does return?" he said to himself. He tossed and turned and wondered and wished, and soon he thought of an idea.

Next day he went to the market and bought some olives. Then he took the gold and the old olives from the jar, and filled the jar up with the new olives. He covered the top of the jar again, and put it back where Ali had left it. The gold he took into his bedroom, where he hid it in a cupboard.

A few days later there was a knock at the door of his house. The merchant opened it, and there outside stood Ali.

"Hello," said Ali. "I've come for my jar of olives. I hope it hasn't been in your way."

"Oh, no, it's been no trouble to me," replied the merchant. "You may take it from my storeroom. You'll find it just where you left it."

So Ali carried the jar to the inn where he was staying. He opened the jar and took out the olives from the top. There, beneath them, were more olives. He took those out too, expecting to see the glitter of gold beneath them. But he saw only more olives. Feeling puzzled, he tipped the jar upside down. More olives rolled out, until they were all upon the floor. There was no gold at all—not one single piece.

"This must be the wrong jar," he thought, but when he looked more carefully at it, he knew that it was not the wrong jar. For a moment he didn't know what to think. Then he said aloud,

"Surely my friend, whom I trusted, hasn't stolen my gold from me!"

Once again he knocked at the merchant's door. The merchant was expecting this, so he had planned what to say, but he pretended to look surprised.

"What's brought you back so soon?" he asked.

"I've come about the jar of olives," replied Ali. "I know it's the same jar that I left in your storeroom, but I left a thousand pieces of gold in with the olives, and now I can't find them."

"I haven't touched your jar!" exclaimed the merchant angrily. "You left it in my care for seven years. You found it just where you had left it. Now you come and ask me for a thousand pieces of gold! I wonder you don't ask me for diamonds or pearls!"

People passing in the street heard the sound of their loud, angry voices, and drew near to listen. So very soon everyone in the town knew that Ali accused the merchant of stealing a thousand pieces of gold which were hidden in a jar of olives. Even the children began to talk about it.

Ali was unhappy because the merchant had been a bad friend to him, and he was angry because now he had no money. So he told his story to the king, and asked that the king should judge between the merchant and himself. The king agreed to do this, and commanded them both to come before him on the following day.

That evening the king dressed himself as a poor man, and wandered through the streets of the town, listening to different people talking. Nearly everyone was talking about Ali and the merchant.

"The merchant *must* have stolen the gold," said some.

"But how can it be proved?" asked others.

"That's just the trouble," thought the king to himself. "How can it be proved?"

At that moment he came upon a group of children playing at the side of the path. He stood back in the shadows and listened to their game. Strangely enough, they were playing at Ali and the merchant, and one boy was sitting on the ground pretending to be the king.

"Ali," he was saying, "let me see the jar of olives which you left with the merchant for seven years."

The child who was supposed to be Ali handed him

a jar, and the boy-king looked inside it.

"These are fine olives," he remarked, pretending to eat one. Then he stopped suddenly, and said, puzzled, "Surely olives would be bad after seven years!"

"Ah!" thought the king. "There's the proof I need."

Next day Ali and the merchant went before the king, and a crowd of people gathered round to listen. Ali told his story again, and the merchant said once more that he had not touched the olives.

"Ali," said the king, "let me see the jar of olives."

Ali handed it to the king, and the king looked inside.

"These are fine olives," said the king, tasting one. "I didn't know olives could be kept for seven years, and still be good."

He turned to a messenger, and said,

"Bring me an olive merchant."

After a few moments an olive merchant was brought forward.

"Tell me," said the king. "How long will olives keep, and still be good to eat?"

The olive merchant bowed low, and replied in a grave voice,

"Not more than two years, Your Majesty. By the third year they will have no taste and no colour."

"Then," said the king, "look at these olives, and tell me how long it is since they were put into this jar."

The merchant looked, tasted the olives, and answered, "They're good olives, new this year, Your Majesty."

"But Ali says he put them in the jar seven years ago, and this merchant here says that he hasn't touched them in all that time," said the king.

"No, Your Majesty," said the olive merchant. "These olives have been picked this year. Anyone will tell you the same."

So it was proved that Ali's olives had been taken out of the jar, and changed for new ones. Only the merchant could have changed them, and therefore he must have taken the gold as well. He was ordered to return the thousand pieces of gold to Ali, which he did—every one.

As for the boy who had pretended to be the king in the game of the night before, he was surprised and delighted when a messenger from the palace knocked at his door, and gave him a purse with a hundred pieces of gold inside it.

"This," said the messenger, "is a present from the king—for a very clever boy."

Adapted

A goldcrest

Did You Know This?

A lapwing on its nest.

If you approach a lapwing's nest, the bird will sometimes hop away, pretending to have a broken wing. It does this so that you will look at it or follow it, instead of walking on and perhaps finding its eggs or its young ones.

The goldcrest or golden-crested wren, which is one of the smallest British birds, weighs only 28 grams. But this wren is a determined little bird, and every year it crosses the North Sea during migration. No doubt it knows when the right wind is blowing, and is able to decide upon the best time to make the long sea crossing.

Other birds of course travel thousands of kilometres during their flights from cold countries to warmer lands for the winter.

Some birds lay eggs that are almost the exact colouring of their surroundings. So even when you are almost on top of the eggs, you find it difficult to see them, because they are so much like the earth or the stones or the bushes.

When salmon are swimming, they sometimes jump waterfalls, in order to continue their journey upstream.

The lobster is rather clever. If an enemy seizes hold of one of its legs, the lobster casts off the leg that is caught. It doesn't seem to come to any harm by doing this, and it is able to hurry away to a place of safety.

Have you ever wondered how pearls are made? A little piece of sand or grit finds its way into an oyster shell. The oyster is irritated by this and sends out a fluid called nacre, which flows over the sand or grit, and covers it. In this way a pearl is formed.

(*left*) A salmon leaping a waterfall. (*above*) A lobster on the sea-bed. (*right*) A pearl in an oyster shell.

Deno All Alone

Deno lived in a lighthouse with her mother and father. It was made of stone, and built on a bank of small stones, with the light fixed high on the top of a steel tower. There was sea all round, but land wasn't far away, and whenever food and coal and oil were running low, the family would go across to the town by rowing boat to do the shopping.

Deno liked going to town, and playing and talking for a while with her friends, and perhaps taking a turn at the oars on the way home. But she liked the loneliness of the lighthouse too, with the gulls that flew by in the daytime, and the light that shone out at night. She knew how important it was that the lamp should be kept burning through the hours of darkness, flashing its warning to ships at sea.

Now Deno's birthday was in March, and every year when it drew near, there was, of course, very special shopping for her mother and father to do when they went to town.

But one year March was wild and stormy. The waves thundered up on the beach in foaming anger, and the sea-gulls screamed and cried and flew away to the land. The wind howled round the lighthouse, and the sea tossed and roared.

"We can't go ashore today," said Deno's father. "Perhaps the weather will be better tomorrow."

He said this many times, but days and days went by, and still the storm continued.

A week passed. The food in the house was beginning to get low.

"We mustn't eat so much," said Deno's mother with a smile.

"The weather is sure to change soon," said her father. "Tomorrow perhaps." But it did not change.

Eight days passed—nine days, ten days, eleven days—two weeks. Mother and Father ate less and less, so that there should be food enough for Deno. Deno's birthday came, and still the rowing boat couldn't cross the angry sea. So instead of a special birthday tea, with all sorts of nice things to eat, there was scarcely anything on the table at all.

Every day the family watched the sea. If the waves would quieten down just for a little while, the rowing boat could be taken across.

Then came a day when the only food left in the house was half a loaf of bread. There was not a scrap of anything else.

"We'll *have* to go today," said Deno's father. Anxiously he watched and waited for a chance. The sea was as high as ever, but later on it sank back a little, and the wind wasn't quite so strong.

"Now!" he said.

He had decided that his wife should go with him to help carry the provisions to the boat, but that Deno should stay at home.

"We won't be long," said Deno's mother with a wave of her hand. The little boat was launched, and bravely it set off across the strip of sea.

When Mother and Father reached the shore, they quickly collected their food, oil and coal, and hurried back to the beach with it. At any moment the gale might grow stronger again. There was no time to spare. But as they ran to the place where they had left the boat, they saw that they were too late. The wind was blowing more strongly than before, and the waves were greater and more terrible than they had been all through the month. No little boat could sail on such a sea.

There were some fishermen standing near.

"You can't possibly go back today," they said.

"But I must!" cried the lighthouse keeper. "I must light the lamp. Besides, Deno is all alone out there, and she's hungry."

"Try my motor boat," said someone, so the food was packed into that. But even the motor boat couldn't travel in the storm. It was tossed from one wave to another and would have been swamped and lost if it had tried to go any further.

Sadly Deno's mother and father stood on the shore again. They knew that they would be drowned if they tried to go through that sea. They gazed across at the lighthouse. They could see it, but they couldn't get to it. Deno was all alone out there, and she was hungry, and when darkness came, the light wouldn't be lit. How many ships might be lost in the storm without the light to guide them?

Meanwhile Deno was curled up in a chair, reading a book. It was an interesting book, so the time passed quickly. She felt very hungry at dinner time—but never mind. Mother and Father would soon be back with plenty of food, and oh, what a feast they would have then!

Afternoon came, but Mother and Father didn't come back. Deno knew they wouldn't visit friends today. She knew they would come back as quickly as possible, before the storm grew worse. She put down her book, and looked out of the window.

The storm *had* grown worse. Oh, dear! It was worse than it had been all the past three weeks. Waves crashed on the shore with the noise of thunder. The air was filled with the mist of splashing spray. A lonely sea-gull battled against the wind, and then dropped helplessly on the stones. Even a sea-gull, with its powerful wings, couldn't fly in such a gale. Certainly a little boat wouldn't be able to sail. Deno knew that Mother and Father couldn't possibly get back that night.

"Oh, dear," she said aloud, "I'm *so* hungry." Oh, well, she could eat up the half loaf. She would have a good meal tomorrow when Mother and Father came home, and a fire to keep her warm as well. She cut a slice of bread, and while she was eating it, she started cutting another. Then she thought,

"Perhaps I'd better *not* eat it all—just in case—"

The afternoon passed slowly, and daylight began to fade. Deno had a drink of water, just for something to do.

"I'll go to bed very early, before it gets dark, and I'll lie in bed and read," she said to herself. "I'll keep warmer that way, and perhaps I'll finish my book."

Then a thought came to her. It came so suddenly that she stopped, with the cup held to her lips.

"The light! What about the light? *I'll* have to keep it burning. I'd better see to it quickly before dark." She put on her thickest sweater and set out.

This was no easy lighthouse, where she would have to walk up a winding staircase, and turn on a switch. Oh, no. This was a lamp that burned oil. The glass had to be kept clean and shining. The wick had to be trimmed. The lamp had to be kept filled with oil. And to light it, she would have to climb up an iron ladder outside the tower, up and up in the wind and spray; and at the top there was a heavy iron door to open. She would have to climb through the doorway and light the lamp. It was not an easy job. Even Father found it hard work in bad weather.

Deno was cold and hungry, and as she went out of the door of the house, the wind rushed at her with such force that she could scarcely breathe. She struggled to the ladder, held on tightly to the rails, and started to climb. The higher she climbed, the harder it became. Her clothes flapped against her legs. Spray filled her eyes, and half blinded her. The wind blew so fiercely, so wildly that she had to cling on with all her might, and all the time the waves broke on the stones with a deafening roar.

What a long way up it seemed. What a *long* way! She felt strange because she was so hungry. Her hands were *so* cold, and her lips tasted salty like the sea.

What a long way, up and up and up, through the spray and the wind.

At last she reached the top. There was the iron door in front of her eyes. She had only to open it and climb through. At least it would be sheltered from the wind, there inside with the lamp. She turned the handle and pulled the door. It didn't move. It was heavy—made of iron—and the wind was blowing against it. She pulled and pulled. Once it opened just a crack, and slammed shut again. Even Father had a job to open it in windy weather. So how could Deno possibly do it—all alone?

She pulled again. She pulled and pulled.

"I'll have to leave it," she said to herself at last, "I won't be able to light the lamp."

She rested a moment, clinging to the ladder far,

far above the sea, and there came into her mind the thought of ships out in the storm. Soon it would be dark, quite dark. Sailors would be looking for the lighthouse beam. How would they find their way without the light to guide them? If she didn't light the lamp, ships might be wrecked tonight. She *must* light the lamp. She *must*.

The short rest had given her new strength. Once more she pulled and pulled at the iron door, and this time it opened.

Away on the shore, her mother and father were worrying about her, and worrying about the light. It wouldn't be lit tonight, and ships would be lost in the storm. Darkness was falling now, and the lighthouse was hidden in cloud and mist. Sadly they looked across the angry water, and suddenly, as they looked, a beam of light shone out, clearly, brightly. Deno had lit the lamp, and all night long it flashed its warning to ships at sea.

* * * * * *

Morning came, and still the storm raged. Several brave fishermen tried to get boats out to the lighthouse, but again they failed. Everyone knew that Deno must be weak with hunger, yet no one could do anything to help her. Yet when night came, the light shone out bravely across the water once more. Deno had lit the lamp for the second time.

The next day the same thing happened. The storm raged. Boats tried to reach the lighthouse and failed. Mother and Father were almost ill with worry. Deno must be starving—simply starving! Yet for a third night the lighthouse beam flashed across the sea, warning and guiding ships in the storm. For a third time, in spite of cold and hunger, and wind and spray, Deno had managed somehow to light the lamp.

Morning came once more. Still the storm raged. For three days and nights now, Deno had been all alone. Would no one ever come to help her? Would Mother and Father never get through the gale, and bring food for her and oil for the lamp? She was hungry, so hungry, and the oil for the lamp was low, so low. To Deno it all seemed like a strange lonely dream, that went on and on, day and night.

Suddenly, in the afternoon, she saw a boat. Then a mighty wave rose, and hid it from view. Perhaps it hadn't been a boat at all. Then it appeared again.

It was the lifeboat, with all the lifeboat crew, and her mother and father in it!

"Oh!" whispered Deno. "At last! At last!"

Anxiously she pressed her face to the window, watching the boat battle with the waves. Oh! It couldn't land! The waves just played with it as if it were a toy. Wildly the wind blew, and the sea thundered. Up in the spray went the lifeboat, and then down in the depths of the waves. Up again and down again, up and down, up and down.

"Oh!" murmured Deno. "Will they ever do it?"

Then there was the crunching sound of wood on stones. Several of the crew were jumping waist deep, shoulder deep, into the water. The lifeboat was landing! Mother and Father were climbing out, with food and coal and oil. Mother and Father were home again. Deno was saved.

If you ever go to the Isle of Wight for a holiday, and visit Bembridge, you may see the lighthouse where Deno lived. Everyone called her Deno, but her real name was Ethel Langton.

Perhaps when it's dark, you will see the light flashing out across the sea, and then you will remember how brave Deno kept it burning for three stormy nights when she was all alone.

Do You Know?

Some Spiders Have Parachutes

Have you ever noticed that some mornings when you go outside, there are long fine silky threads on the ground and even in the air? These silky threads look just like those used by spiders in spinning their webs. You wonder and perhaps say to yourself, "It seems as though a lot of broken spider's webs have been blown all over the place." What are these white threads that glisten in the morning dew, and look almost like frost on the ground and the bushes? Their real name is *gossamer*, and they are the threads spun by the tiny gossamer spider.

When the sun is shining and the air is warm, this tiny spider spins one or two threads on a twig or a branch. Then it holds tightly on to these fine threads and sends out some silvery streamers from its body. It uses these streamers as a parachute and jumps off into the air, with its silken parachute flying out behind it. On a windy morning the tiny spider, with many other friends, is blown along over the fields.

Some of the threads of these tiny fliers catch on the bushes or fall to the ground, and that is what we see glistening in the dew in the early morning.

The spiders are so light that they can float along for quite a distance, leaving little pieces of their parachutes here and there.

The Story of Ships

There has been water on earth since the world began—fast flowing rivers, still calm lakes, and wide tossing seas. And as long as there have been people upon the earth, men have wondered where the rivers flowed, what was across the lakes, and whether there were other lands over the seas. This is why boats were made.

The first boat was nothing but a floating log, with a cave boy lying face downwards on it, paddling himself along with his hands. Logs roll over easily, and the boy must have fallen in the water many times before he found that it was easier to manage a tree trunk which was hollowed out from one side. So his next boat was a dug-out canoe. He made it by burning out or cutting away the inside of a tree trunk, using his simple flint tools to smooth and shape it, and taking pieces of flat wood for paddles.

At about the same time someone made a raft, by binding several logs together. This kept afloat very well, but was more difficult to steer.

No one knows exactly what the first sail was like. Perhaps, on a hot day, a boy, floating on his father's raft, took off the animal skin he wore and held it up in his arms. The wind caught it and tried to blow it away. It was a game to the boy, and he held on tightly as the skin flapped in his hands. His father noticed that the raft was moving much faster than usual. He looked round, and saw that the force of the wind against his son's animal skin was sending the raft along.

It seemed a good idea. That day he made a mast from a tall, slim tree, and he fixed up a sail of skin.

People in different parts of the world had different ideas about making boats.

They tried floating on large bundles of reeds.

They made boats, kept up by bags of straw or sheepskins filled with air.

They used boats that had logs at the side to balance them. These were hollowed-out tree trunks with two long poles fixed across them, and joined to floating logs at the sides.

They made coracles, round in shape, woven of wicker like baskets, and covered with skin.

From these small and strange beginnings of long ago grew the great sailing ships of later days—ships with square, painted sails, and oarsmen ready to row when the wind failed—ships with wooden models of men, women, lions, dragons or birds carved on the prow—ships with eyes painted on the front to help them to "see".

A single square sail hanging across the ship could of course be used only when the wind blew from the back, but gradually other sails came into use. First a small extra one was added at the front, and later sails were rigged up lengthways of the ship, fore and aft, to catch the wind whichever way it was blowing.

Sailing ships became better and better as the years went by, till they reached the height of their glory in the ships known as clippers and windjammers. What a wonderful sight it must have been when one of these sped over the sea, with the wind billowing out its great, white sails, and the sun gleaming on the blue water. People thought that no ship of the future could ever look more lovely, or sail more swiftly. But sailing ships, however well made, could not travel in calm weather, and there were many days when no wind blew.

Paddles fixed on water wheels were tried next, and then came steam. Several ships were fitted with steam engines, but were used only on lakes and rivers. Many people laughed at them, and said they would never be made to work properly. Others were terrified of the noise, and the smoke and the sparks blowing out of the funnels. After a while, bigger steamships were made, and tested on sea voyages, but they usually had sails as well, in case the engines failed.

Until then ships had been made of wood. Any piece of wood thrown upon water will at once float. Iron, of course, sinks. Yet shipbuilders learned the secret of shaping iron in such a way that it would float. So ships of iron were built to take the place of ships of wood.

Steamships needed to carry a great deal of coal for the engines, and the coal took up large spaces that might have been used for cargo. But they could go very much faster than any ship of the past, and year by year they were made bigger, more comfortable, and faster still.

Then once more a new kind of ship appeared, a ship

(*above*) An ocean liner—the *Queen Elizabeth 2*.
(*below*) A hovercraft.

that needed no coal but used oil to drive its engine. Oil takes less space than coal, and ships are able to carry enough to last for long voyages.

Today there are ocean liners that are like small towns. They have shops and swimming pools on board, and rooms and cabins for thousands of people. Today too, there are ferries and hovercraft that take cars across the Channel. There are aircraft carriers and warships. There are racing boats and tankers, lifeboats

(*above*) An oil tanker—the SS *Darina*.
(*below*) The Stornoway lifeboat.

and submarines. On every sea, day and night, there are ships. In every harbour, lights flash and flags fly, and some sailor gazes at new land for the first time.

The cave boy who floated down the river on a log started one of the longest stories in the world, the Story of Ships. But he did not know the end of the story.

Neither do we.

The Story of a Road

Once upon a time, hundreds of years ago, there was a little footpath. It was rough, narrow and stony. The only people who used it were the farmer taking his cows to the meadow and the children wandering round the side of the hill, on their way to the village. But as the years went by, the path became a little flatter where the cows' hooves wore it down, and a little wider where the children ran over the edge of it.

Not far away stood a castle where a rich man lived. He had two castles—a winter one and a summer one. It was time now to go to the summer one, so all his family and his servants began to prepare for the journey.

The rich man had noticed the footpath getting wider and smoother, and he said,

"We'll go that way this time. It will make our journey much shorter."

So very soon the little footpath felt the trotting of horses' feet, and the rumbling of wooden wheels. It felt proud to think that so many grand people were riding along on it.

The rich man was dressed in beautiful clothes of scarlet and blue, and the horse on which he rode had a purple cloth on its back. Two servants rode beside him, and seven more followed. Then came a carriage the colour of gold, with the rich man's wife and his four little children jogging up and down inside it.

After that came oxen pulling three slow, creaking carts filled with luggage, and then came seven more servants on prancing horses. The sun shone on the cloths of blue and scarlet, and on the purple tassels that hung from the horses' heads. It danced on the golden carriage, dazzling the eyes of the little village boys and girls, who stopped to stare in wonder. It was like the procession of a king!

In those days people didn't travel unless they had a good reason. In the winter, roads were flooded by rain. Wagons stuck in the mud, and their wheels made great ruts and holes. People were likely to lose their way, and often there were animals and robbers about.

It was the journey of the rich man and his family that really changed the little footpath from a footpath to a road. The horses' hooves scattered the dust. The wooden wheels flattened down the grass at the sides.

Next day a pedlar, trudging along the highroad with a bag of pretty things to sell, looked across the grass, and noticed the path beyond the castle.

"Ah!" he said. "A short cut! I'll go this way."

Then a company of merchants passed along, on

horseback. The horses carried bundles of cloth to be sold; and small bells jingled to warn people of their coming.

So the footpath became wide and worn, and more and more people used it. Minstrels passed that way, humming the tunes they meant to play upon their pipes at inns and castles. Jugglers and dancers went to earn some money at the village fair. Messengers carried letters.

The road was made wider still, and bushes at the side were cut down. No longer was it a little footpath that hardly anyone used. It was a busy highway.

The village became more important too, with so many people passing through it. The innkeeper had to put more beds in his inn, and his wife was kept very busy cooking meals for hungry travellers. Each day as the sun sank to rest, bells rang out from the church, and a pot of fire was hung up in the tower to guide people who still wandered in the dark.

For years and years the road wound its way round the side of the hill. In summer it was rough and stony and dusty. In winter parts of it were washed away by rain, or buried beneath snow. Sometimes a farmer filled up a few of the holes, or the people of the church dug a ditch at the side to drain the water away. But apart from this, no one ever bothered to keep the road in good repair. Yet still the traffic went on, round the hill, and into the village.

It would take too long to tell of all the feet that walked, and all the wheels that rolled along the highway. Carts and wagons and carriages changed. People's clothes and ideas changed. And the years passed by, until five hundred years had gone.

Then came a man called John McAdam. He brought workmen and tools. He straightened the road, cutting away some of the twists and turns. He built a new smooth surface to it, like a strong, solid floor, that could bear heavy weights.

By that time people travelled by stage coach, drawn by horses. The coach was gaily painted, and had the names of the places to which it went, written on the door. The driver sat high up at the front. Some passengers sat inside the coach, and others outside. The horses galloped for sixteen kilometres, and were then taken to the stable of an inn, to rest. Different horses were obtained, and the coach continued its journey.

On John McAdam's roads, stage coaches could travel much faster. Wheels could whirl round swiftly.

Horses could gallop like the wind. Each driver tried to go faster still, faster than any other driver in the country. People who had long journeys to make were scarcely given time to eat their dinner when the stage coach stopped at an inn.

"Ready!" the coachman would call, blowing his horn to show that he was just starting off again. Half the food would be left uneaten on the plates. The people would scramble into the coach, and the fresh horses would pull it on its way.

More and more stage coaches used the road, wheels whirring, horses galloping, faster, faster, faster.

And then one year the road saw a strange puffing coach in the distance where the rich man's castle had once been. George Stephenson was building trains. Engines were driven by steam and did not have to rest like horses. They were faster than stage coaches, or anything else on the road.

People who had to travel now travelled by train. The stage coaches disappeared altogether. Some were left to fall to pieces in stable yards. Others were used by farmers as houses for hens. No one seemed to want the road any more. Bushes grew nearer and blocked the way. Grass crept over the edges, and weeds pushed up through McAdam's fine road. The busy highway began to look like the little footpath it had been five hundred years ago.

"My days are over," thought the road. "No one needs me now."

Only the birds flew above it, and little wild rabbits chased each other across it.

For fifty years the road slept.

Then one day it was awakened by a strange sound. A man was walking along, holding a red flag. Behind him came a queer snorting thing on wheels.

"A stage coach at last," thought the road, but it wasn't a stage coach, for it wasn't pulled by horses. It just seemed to go by itself, jerking, banging, rattling.

A crowd of people followed. They laughed and pointed and chattered. They had come to watch the first motor car they had ever seen.

* * * * * *

The road still winds round the side of the hill, and all day long a stream of traffic passes by. There are cars and caravans, buses and lorries—hurrying, overtaking each other, speeding along the fine modern road—faster, faster and faster.

The road now has scarcely a moment in which to remember the children who stopped to stare at the first slow, golden carriage, or the minstrels, the jugglers and the dancers going to the fair, or the merchants and the messengers of six hundred years ago. Only sometimes, when the night is dark, and the late motor cars have flashed their headlamps and whizzed by, it hears again the jingling of bells, the clatter of horses' hooves, and the blowing of the stage coach horn. As it winds round the hillside, white and shining in the blackness, it dreams of days of long ago.

Do You Know?

How High a Hare Can Jump?

Perhaps you have seen a hare bounding away across the fields, and perhaps you have thought that it is very much like its cousin the rabbit. It is in some ways, but the rabbit is born with closed eyes and no fur, and the hare is born with its eyes open, and some fur on its body.

The rabbit spends most of its early life down in a burrow in the earth, but the young hare, or leveret as it is called, lives in a shallow hollow in the open ground.

(*left*) A hare running away to safety. Notice its long back legs.
(*above*) These leverets are about two days old. They are not easy to see in their grassy hollow.

As the young hare grows a little older, it looks rather handsome in its reddish-brown coat, and it soon becomes very good at jumping. It can jump over quite large things, and has even been known to jump right over a small motor car.

Have you ever noticed that the front legs of a hare are much shorter than the back legs? So although it can run very quickly uphill, it has to run downhill in a zigzag fashion, to prevent itself from overbalancing.

As well as being a swift runner and a high jumper, it is also a good swimmer. It can cross a pool or a river, or even swim in the sea.

Where the Eyes of a Flatfish Are?

The eyes of a flatfish (such as a flounder or a plaice) are both on the upper side of the body. This is because these fish spend much of their time lying flat on the bed of the sea. But their eyes have not always been in that position.

When a flatfish is born, it looks like an ordinary fish, and has one eye on each side of its body in the usual way. When it is about a month old, it turns over and starts swimming on one side, and becomes much flatter. Then the eye from one side gradually moves over until it is close to the eye on the other side, and there it stays.

Bjorn Borg

"He's done it! He's won! Borg is the champion—for the fifth time!"

The whole crowd at Wimbledon burst into cheers. People rose to their feet, waved and shouted "Bravo! Bravo!"

Down below, on the famous Centre Court, the tall blonde Swede, his hair held in place by the familiar headband, sank to his knees.

Then he rose and went over to shake hands with John McEnroe, the defeated finalist.

It was Saturday, the fifth of July 1980. The match had taken three hours fifty-four minutes. Borg won 1-6, 6-5, 6-3, 6-7 (16-18), 8-6.

Afterwards, Borg said,

"My biggest ambition is to be remembered as the greatest player of all time...."

But Borg wasn't just a great tennis player. He was a great sportsman. Sometimes things went badly for him. But he never shouted at the umpire or lost his temper. So he was a popular player as well as a star.

How did it all begin?

Bjorn Borg was born on the sixth of June 1956 in Sodertalje, a little town in Sweden.

Like most Swedes, Bjorn's family loved sport. His father was a major table tennis player. Young Bjorn learned to play almost as soon as he could hold a bat. At home the family used to play a sort of ping-pong, using a row of books as a net.

But it was ice hockey that Bjorn really loved. He

was only nine when he played for the town's junior team.

"Maybe," he said, "I can play for Sweden when I grow up."

He was the fastest player in the junior team. He was very strong too. A good ice hockey player must be both fast and strong.

But all that changed. When Bjorn was nine years old, his father won the city table tennis championship. His prize was a tennis racket. He took the racket home and gave it to his son.

"Here," he said with a smile, "this is for you."

Bjorn couldn't wait to learn to play. Next morning he got up very early, and with his new racket, he went off to join the local club.

"I'm sorry," said the club manager. "The beginners' class is full. You'll have to wait."

Bjorn was bitterly disappointed. He didn't want to wait. He wanted to learn to play tennis right away. But he didn't give up. Instead, he went home and practised by himself, hitting a tennis ball against the garage wall. Day after day he practised until at last the longed-for message came from the tennis club. There was now a vacancy. Young Bjorn could join the beginners' class.

He went to the club every day. He practised hard for hours on end—sometimes until late at night. In Sweden the summer days are long and it is light almost round the clock.

Soon it was clear that Bjorn was a natural tennis player. But he still enjoyed ice hockey, and to train for the ice hockey team he practised lifting weights.

He said himself,

"It's good if you can play a lot of sports when you're young, and then when you're older, choose just one."

It wasn't long before he had to choose just one sport to follow.

He won his first tennis tournament when he was only eleven. By the time he was thirteen, he was competing in the Swedish National Championships. At fourteen, he was chosen to play for Sweden in a junior tournament in Germany.

A little sadly, he decided that the time had come to give up ice hockey. From then on he would play only tennis.

When Bjorn was fifteen, in 1972, he decided he wanted to leave school so that he could concentrate on playing tennis. At first, the headmaster refused. "You're too young to leave school," he said. But Bjorn's parents and a top tennis coach talked to the headmaster and at last it was agreed. Bjorn would leave school and after that tennis would be his whole life.

Later that year he was chosen to play in the Davis Cup against New Zealand. The young Swede was to play against New Zealand's number one player. He lost the first two sets. He was losing 3-1 in the third.

Then his coach gave him a lighter racket. After that Bjorn won five games in a row—and the next two sets. At only fifteen, he was the youngest player to win a Davis Cup match.

Bjorn became popular with the crowds who watched him because he was always calm. He never seemed to get cross or out of temper. But he says it wasn't always so. At fifteen and sixteen, he remembers, he used to throw tantrums. He has told of one match when he lost his temper and shouted at the umpire.

"In front of TV cameras, I questioned a call," he said. He remembers how he strode over to the side of the court. He drew a circle round the mark where the ball had hit the ground. But the umpire was firm.

Bjorn lost the point. He was so upset he couldn't concentrate and he lost the match. "That was the last display of poor sportsmanship of my career," he says. From that day, he never again showed anger or disappointment at an umpire's decision.

Bjorn played all over the world in top class tournaments. He played in the Davis Cup for Sweden, he played in the French championships. And then, in 1973, he reached the quarter finals at Wimbledon. "A Star is Bjorn!" said the headlines.

He had played at Wimbledon before. In 1972 he had won the junior title. But by this time he was becoming famous.

The next year, 1974, he was the number three player in the world. He won both the French and Italian championships. He was only eighteen. However, at Wimbledon that year, he reached only the third round.

Still, Borg was on the way up and by this time he was winning a great deal of prize money. So he decided to become a professional player. That meant he could play all the year round in exhibition matches all over the world.

In 1975 Bjorn and his parents moved from Sweden

to the Mediterranean and settled in the tiny principality of Monaco. There, with the help of his parents, Bjorn opened a sports shop.

In 1975 he won the French championship again and in the same year he reached the quarter finals at Wimbledon.

He first won the Wimbledon championship in 1976, when he was twenty. He said afterwards,

"I was not supposed to win, so there was no pressure. I just hit away and it seemed impossible to miss."

In the final against Ilie Nastase, Bjorn lost the first three games.

"I remember being scared I wouldn't win a game," he says, "and being the first person to lose a Wimbledon final 6-0, 6-0, 6-0. Then I started to relax."

Finally, he won 6-4, 6-2, 9-7.

Bjorn won Wimbledon again in 1977, 1978, 1979 — and in 1980, ranked as number one player in the world, he won for the fifth time. He was without doubt the greatest player in the world.

Soon after the 1980 Wimbledon tournament, Bjorn was married. His wife, Mariana Simionescu, was a Rumanian tennis player. She had been French junior champion and had reached the last sixteen at Wimbledon. They were married in Rumania in a village near Bucharest.

In 1981, Bjorn was back at Wimbledon. But in this year he lost the final to John McEnroe.

Soon after that, in 1982, he announced that he would not play at Wimbledon again. He was going to retire.

He was still only twenty-six when he played his last major tournament at Monaco in April 1983.

Although he was beaten, the crowds still cheered him as if he were a champion.

Borg said he had decided some months earlier, while practising in Stockholm, to give up tennis.

"I'll still play tennis," he said, "but not in competitions. I don't enjoy it any more. I want to set other goals."

For ten years he had been at the top.

"During these ten years," he said, "I had fun. I loved it." But now he had realised that there was life outside the tennis courts.

* * * * * *

What made him the world's greatest player? Some say he was the greatest player of all time.

Gene Scott, the editor of *Tennis Week*, says,

"He never appears to be moving quickly, and yet he's never out of position."

Others say, "He's the best athlete in tennis," and, "Every stroke is the right one."

Ilie Nastase, who lost to Bjorn in the 1976 Wimbledon Championship, joked, "They should send Bjorn away to another planet. We play tennis. He plays something else."

Another player said simply, "We're all playing against a legend."

But there have been other great players. Why was Bjorn Borg so popular with the crowds? Why did people queue all night to watch him play? Why did the packed Centre Court at Wimbledon cheer him until they were hoarse?

Maybe it's because he wasn't just a great player. He was a great sportsman too. He never lost his temper or behaved badly. He was always fair and generous to other players.

The nine-year-old boy hitting a tennis ball against the garage wall had come a long way. He was the greatest player in the world.

Anne Forsyth